D1631325

a
b

KNOWABOUT

Capacity

© 1994 Watts Books

Watts Books
96 Leonard Street
London EC2A 4RH

Franklin Watts Australia
14 Mars Road
Lane Cove
NSW 2066

ISBN: 0 7496 1668 7

Dewey Decimal Classification 530.8

10 9 8 7 6 5 4 3 2 1

A CIP catalogue record for this book
is available from the British Library.

Editor: Ruth Thomson
Assistant Editor: Annabel Martin

Design: Chloë Cheesman

Additional photographs:
Viewfinder 29; ZEFA 22, 26.

Printed in Hong Kong

KNOWABOUT

Capacity

Text: Henry Pluckrose
Photography: Chris Fairclough

Watts Books

London • New York • Sydney

Have you ever played with damp sand, packed it into a bucket ...

and made a sand castle?

Why does the sand

take the shape of the bucket?

A bucket, a thimble, an egg cup,
a jar and a box are containers.
Containers hold things.
Inside a container there is a space.

The space inside a container can hold solids, liquids or just air.

Here are some containers.
If you filled each of them
with water ...

can you guess which would hold the most,
and which would hold the least?

It is easy to guess which container
will hold the most water
when they are different sizes.

It's much more difficult to guess
when the containers look almost the same!

Guessing can be difficult.

Which of these two containers

holds the most?

We must measure to find out .

Pour water from the jug
into the dish.
What does this tell you?

Now collect some empty containers.
How can you work out
which one will hold the most water
and which one will hold the least?

We do not have to use water.

We could use sand or marbles instead.

The sand fills all the space in the jar.

Do the marbles fill all the space?

Often we need to measure exactly.

We use the litre as the standard measure for liquids.

Drinks are sold by the litre …

and so are many other things.

FOAM
BATH
Mountain
Pine

BATH CARE
FROM
SOMERFIELD
1 litre

Magicote
NON-DRIP GLOSS
BUCKINGHAM
1 litre

SOMERFIELD
Vegetable
oil

Suitable for deep
and shallow frying,
salad dressings
and other
culinary uses.

1 litre e
BEST BEFORE END (2)
BBE JUNE 94 3259 HB

1 Litre e

MON BLO
Fabr
nditi

a softe
fresher u

MER

NEW
ULTRA
Daz
1L

TOTAL
SUPER MULTIGRADE MOTOR OIL
GOLD

FORMULATED FOR ALL MODERN ENGINES
UNBEATABLE ALL YEAR PERFORMANCE
PREVENTS BLACK SLUDGE

1
LITRE

A litre is quite
a large measure.
Smaller quantities are
measured in decilitres
and in millilitres.

30ml
22125
MORNY
LONDON ENGLAND

Ten decilitres make a litre.

A thousand millilitres make a litre.

Standard measures are important.

The ingredients for a cake

have to be mixed in the right quantities.

Garden fertilizers have to be carefully measured.

Medicines must be
measured carefully
when they are made ...

and when we take them.

Standard measures help us to measure exactly.
When a driver buys a litre of petrol
she knows exactly how much she will get –
wherever she buys it.

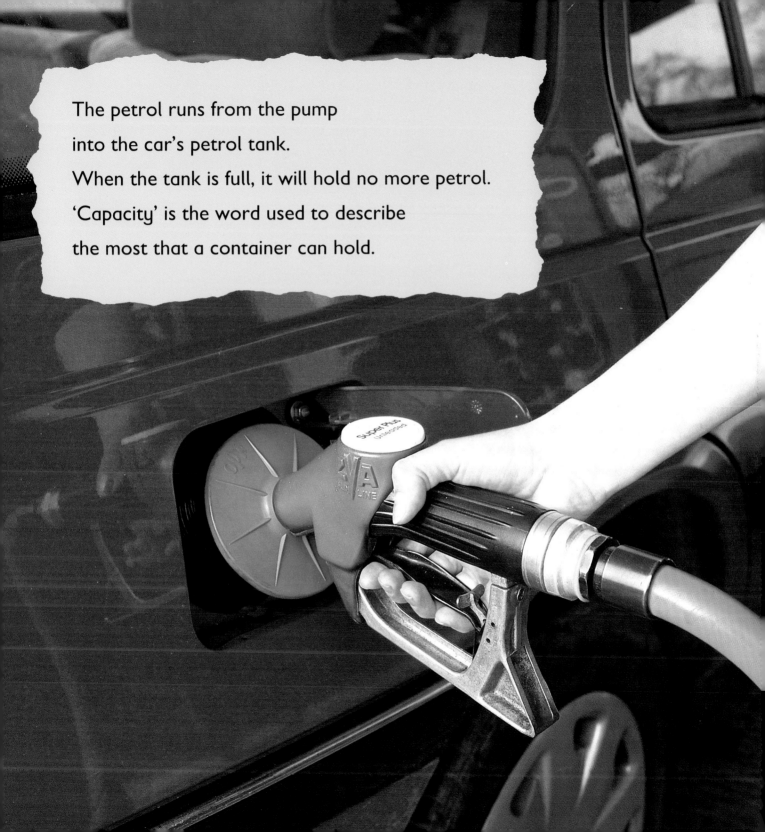

The petrol runs from the pump
into the car's petrol tank.
When the tank is full, it will hold no more petrol.
'Capacity' is the word used to describe
the most that a container can hold.

Some containers are very large.

This chemical tanker holds many litres.

These drums hold chemicals as well.
Which container has the greater capacity –
a tanker or a drum?

Being able to measure capacity is important.
What might happen to this ship if too much coal was loaded into it?

What might happen to this reservoir
if it was overfilled with water?

Capacity is not the same as weight.

The stones fill the jar and so does the water.

Which do you think is heavier?

Capacity is a word we use to describe space —
even when the space is empty!

About this book

This book is designed for use in the home, playgroup and infant school.

Mathematics is a part of the child's world. It is not just about interpreting numbers or in mastering the tricks of addition or multiplication. Mathematics is about *Ideas*. These ideas (or concepts) have been developed over the centuries to help explain particular qualities, such as size, weight, height, as well as relationships and comparisons. Yet all too often the important part which an understanding of mathematics will play in a child's development is forgotten or ignored.

Most adults can solve simple mathematical tasks by "doing them in their head." For example you can probably add up or subtract simple numbers without the need for counters, beads or fingers. Young children find such abstractions almost impossible to master. They need to see, talk, touch and experiment.

The photographs in this book and the text which supports them have been prepared with one major aim. They have been chosen to encourage talk around topics which are essentially mathematical. By talking with you, the young reader will be helped to explore some of the central concepts which underpin mathematics. It is upon an understanding of these concepts that a child's future mastery of mathematics will be built.

Henry Pluckrose